D0490409

IMAGES OF CHRISTMAS

IMAGES OF CHRISTMAS

Dorothy Boux   Eliane Wilson

Bradfield College
Library

CLASS. NO. 230
BOUX

ACC. NO.
A013277

Shepheard – Walwyn
London

This edition © 1984 Dorothy Boux and Eliane Wilson

First published 1984 by
Shepheard ~ Walwyn (Publishers) Ltd.
26, Charing Cross Road
London WC2H ODH

ISBN O 85683 074 7
All rights reserved
Reprinted ~ 1984
Reprinted ~ 1989
Reprinted 1993

Printed and bound in Italy by
A. Mondadori Editore , Verona

To
the children

ACKNOWLEDGEMENTS

We would like to express our gratitude to Sir John Betjeman for allowing us to reproduce his poem 'Christmas', and our grateful thanks to Mrs. G.S.Fraser for her permission to include her husband's poem 'Christmas Letter Home'.

For permission to include poems of which they hold the copyright, grateful acknowledgement is made to the following:

American Heritage Publishing Co. Inc. New York for 'Christmas Dinner at Mount Vernon' from *The American Heritage Cookbook* © 1964.

Associated Book Publishers Ltd. London and E.P. Dutton, New York for A.A. Milne 'King John's Christmas' from *Now We Are Six*.

Jonathan Cape Ltd, London (on behalf of the Estate of Robert Frost) and Holt, Rinehart and Winston Publishers, New York for Robert Frost 'Looking for a Sunset Bird in Winter' and 'Questioning Faces' from *The Poetry of Robert Frost* edited by Edward Connery Lathem.

Andre Deutsch, London for Ogden Nash 'A Carol for Children' from *I Wouldn't Have Missed It*.

Little, Brown and Company, Boston for Ogden

Nash 'A Carol for Children' from *Verses from 1929 On* © 1934.

Faber and Faber, London and Harcourt Brace Jovanovitch, Inc. New York for T. S. Eliot 'Journey of the Magi' from *Collected Poems 1909~1962*

David Higham Associates Limited, London and New Directions, New York for Dylan Thomas 'Conversation about Christmas' from *A Prospect of the Sea*.

Oxford University Press for Gustav Holst music 'Cranham' from *The English Hymnal*.

Penguin Books Ltd. for 'The World's Fair Rose' translated and edited by Elizabeth Poston © 1965 from *The Penguin Book of Christmas Carols*.

The Literary Trustees of Walter de la Mare and the Society of Authors as their representative for Walter de la Mare 'Mistletoe'.

If by inadvertance, copyright material has been included in these pages without permission or if we have failed to trace the publisher, we hope that our sincere apologies will be accepted.

TABLE OF CONTENTS

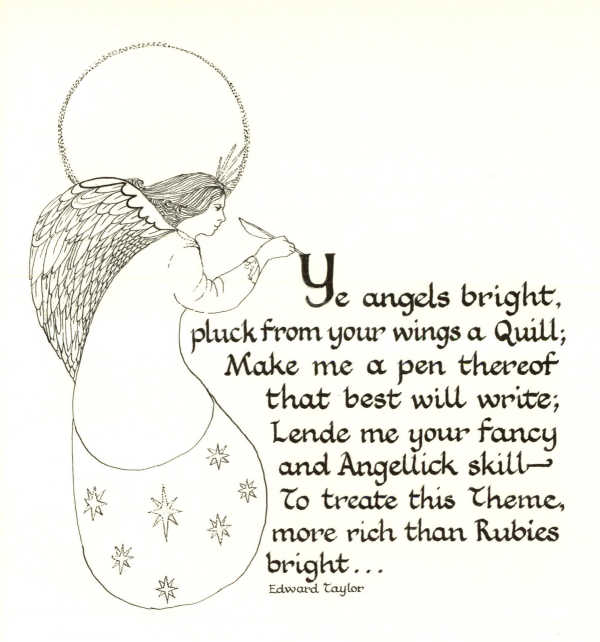

Ye angels bright,
pluck from your wings a Quill;
Make me a pen thereof
that best will write;
Lende me your fancy
and Angellick skill—
To treate this Theme,
more rich than Rubies
bright...
Edward Taylor

For unto us a child is born,
unto us a Son is given:
and the government shall be upon his shoulder:
and his name shall be called Wonderful,
Counseller, The mighty God, The everlasting
Father, The Prince of Peace.

ISAIAH

LOOKING FOR A SUNSET BIRD
IN WINTER

The west was getting out of gold,
The breath of air had died of cold,
When shoeing home across the white,
I thought I saw a bird alight.

In summer when I passed the place
I had to stop and lift my face;
A bird with an angelic gift
Was singing in it sweet and swift.

No bird was singing in it now.
A single leaf was on a bough,
And that was all there was to see
In going twice around the tree.

From my advantage on a hill
I judged that such a crystal chill
Was only adding frost to snow
As gilt to gold that wouldn't show.

A brush had left a crooked stroke
Of what was either cloud or smoke
From north to south across the blue;
A piercing little star was through.

Robert Frost

15

SOME SAY

that ever gainst that season comes
Wherein our Saviours birth is celebrated,
This bird of dawning singeth all night long;
And then, they say no spirit can walk abroad;
The nights are wholesome; then no planets strike,
No fairy takes, nor witch hath power to charm,
So hallowed and so gracious is the time.

WILLIAM SHAKESPEARE

16

THE TIME

draws near the birth of Christ:
The moon is hid; the night is still;
The Christmas bells from hill to hill
Answer each other in the mist.

ALFRED TENNYSON

17

Es ist ein' Ros' entsprungen

The World's Fair Rose

1 Es ist ein' Ros' ent - sprun-gen aus
1. The world's fair Rose has blos-somed Of

ein-er Wur-zel zart, Als uns die Al-ten
Jes-se's roy - al stem Fore - told by an-cient

sun - gen; aus Jes-se kam die Art; und hat ein Blümlein
pro - phets, Who did the news pro - claim; this blos-som greets the

bracht, mit - ten im kal-ten Win -ter, wohl
light. With-in our cold mid - win-ter, up-

zu der hal - ben Nacht.
on our dark mid - night.

18

Das Röslein, das ich meine, davon Jesaias sagt,
Ist Maria die reine, die uns dies Blümlein bracht;
    Aus Gottes ew'gem Rat
    Hat sie ein Kind geboren,
    Ist blieb'n ein' reine Magd.

This Rose, I mean, whose coming, Isaiah first did sing,
Is Mary, pure and blessèd, whose blossom is our King;
    By God's eternal will,
    This Maid who bore her baby
    Is maid and mother still.

Wir bitten dich von Herzen, Maria, Rose zart,
Durch dieses Blümlein's Schmerzen, die er empfunden hat,
    Wollst uns behülflich sein,
    Dass wir ihm mögen machen
    Ein' Wohnung hübsch und fein.

We pray you, Mary mother, the world's fair rose of Grace,
That by your Christchild's passion, we too may see his face;
    So may he help us all
    To offer as his treasure
    Our hearts, his dwelling place.

Michael Praetorius
ELIZABETH POSTON

19

BEHOLD

a woman coming down from the hill country, and she said to me: "Man, whither goest thou?" And I said: "I seek a midwife of the Hebrews." And she answered and said unto me: "Art thou of Israel?" And I said unto her: "Yea." And she said: "And who is she that bringeth forth in the cave?" And I said: "She that is betrothed unto me." And she said to me: "Is she not thy wife?" And I said to her: "It is Mary that was nurtured up in the temple of the Lord: and I received her to wife by lot: and she is not my wife, but she hath conception by the Holy Ghost. And the midwife said unto him:

"Is this the truth?" And Joseph said unto her: "Come hither and see!" And the midwife went with him. And they stood in the place of the cave, and behold a bright cloud overshadowing the cave. And the midwife said: "My soul is magnified this day, because mine eyes have seen marvellous things, for salvation is born unto Israel." And immediately the cloud withdrew itself out of the cave, and a great light appeared in the cave so that our eyes could not endure it. And by little and little withdrew itself until the young child appeared, and went and took the breast of its mother Mary.

ST. JAMES

21

And she brought forth her first~born son~;
and wrapped him in swaddling clothes,
and laid him in a manger, because
there was no room for them in the inn.

SAINT LUKE

CRADLE SONG

William Kirkpatrick

Unison   In moderate time.

way in a— manger, no— crib for a bed—, the lit-tle Lord Je—sus laid— down His sweet head. The stars in the bright sky looked down where He lay— The lit-tle Lord Je-sus a— sleep on the hay.

2. The cattle are lowing, the baby awakes,
    But little Lord Jesus no crying He makes.
    I love Thee, Lord Jesus! Look down from the sky,
    And stay by my bedside till morning is nigh.

3. Be near me, Lord Jesus; I ask Thee to stay
    Close by me for ever and love me, I pray.
    Bless all the dear children in Thy tender care,
    And fit us for heaven, to live with Thee there.

HYMN ON THE MORNING OF CHRIST'S NATIVITY

But peaceful was the night
Wherein the Prince of Light
His reign of peace upon the
earth began:
The winds with wonder whist,
Smoothly the waters kist,
Whispering new joys to the
mild ocean,
Who now hath quite forgot to
rave,
While birds of calm sit
brooding on the charmed wave . . .

JOHN MILTON

A LUTE LULLABY

1. Lul - lay my babe, lie still — and sleep, Soar - it grieves me to
thou be qui - et I'd be glad Weep - ing thus — makes
hear thee weep, Would'st me so sad. My pret-ty lamb,
my pret-ty boy, Sweet-ly sleep, Je-su my Joy. My lit-tle Son,
my lit-tle King, Oh! would'st thou wert peace-ful-ly sleep - ing.

2.
Oh! would'st some angel kiss thy brow,
Sing lullay, sing balalow,
While thus thy lullaby I sing,
Music soothe my sweet lording.
My pretty lamb etc.

3.
What ails my darling thus to cry,
Sing lullay, sing lullaby,
Lie still, my darling rest awhile,
When thou wakest sweetly smile.
My pretty lamb etc.

25

THE OXEN

CHRISTMAS EVE
and twelve of the clock.
'Now they are all on their knees,'
An elder said as we sat in a flock
By the embers in hearthside ease.

We pictured the meek mild creatures where
They dwelt in their strawy pen,
Nor did it occur to one of us there
To doubt they were kneeling then.

So fair a fancy few would weave
In these years! Yet, I feel,
If someone said on Christmas Eve,
'Come,' see the oxen kneel

'In the lonely barton by yonder coomb
Our childhood used to know,'
I should go with him in the gloom,
Hoping it might be so.

THOMAS HARDY

The Shepherd

How sweet is the shepherd's sweet lot.
From the morn to the evening he strays;
He shall follow his sheep all the day,
And his tongue shall be filled with praise.

For he hears the lamb's innocent call
And he hears the ewe's tender reply;
He is watchful while they are in peace
For they know when their shepherd is nigh.

WILLIAM BLAKE

...And there were in the same country
shepherds abiding in the field, keeping
watch over their flock by night.

SAINT LUKE

28

WHILE SHEPHERDS WATCHED

Winchester old

1592

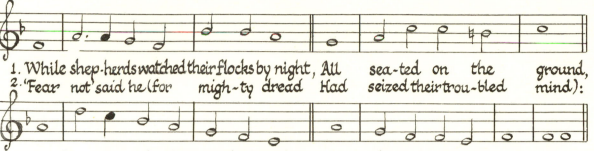

1. While shep-herds watched their flocks by night, All sea-ted on the ground,
2. 'Fear not' said he (for migh-ty dread Had seized their trou-bled mind):

The An-gel of the Lord came down, And glo-ry shone a-rou-nd.
'Glad ti-dings of great joy I bring To you and all man-ki-nd.

3. To you in David's town this day
   Is born of David's line
   A saviour, who is Christ the Lord;
   And this shall be the sign:

4. 'The heavenly babe you there shall find
   To human view displayed,
   All meanly wrapped in swathing bands,
   And in a manger laid.'

5. Thus spake the Seraph, and forthwith
   Appeared a shining throng
   Of Angels praising God, who thus
   Addressed their joyful song.

6. All glory be to God on high,
   And on the earth be peace;
   Good-will henceforth from heaven to men
   Begin and never cease.
                    Nahum Tate

29

THE THREE KINGS

Three Kings came riding from far away,
Melchior and Gaspar and Balthasar;
Three Wise Men out of the East were they,
And they travelled by night and they slept by day
For their guide was a beautiful, wonderful star.

The star was so beautiful, large and clear,
That all the other stars of the sky
Became a white mist in the atmosphere,
And by this they knew that the coming was near
Of the Prince foretold in the prophecy.

Three caskets they bore on their saddle~bows,
Three caskets of gold with golden keys;
Their robes were of crimson silk with rows
Of bells and pomegranates and furbelows,
Their turbans like blossoming almond~trees...

So they rode away; and the star stood still,
The only one in the grey of morn;
Yes, it stopped, it stood still of its own free will,
Right over Bethlehem on the hill,
The city of David, where Christ was born...

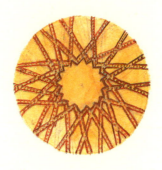

HENRY   WADSWORTH
LONGFELLOW

31

We Three Kings of Orient Are

1. We three kings of O-rient are; Bear-ing gifts we tra-verse a-far, Field and foun-tain, moor and moun-tain, Fol-low-ing yon-der star.

REFRAIN

O — star of won-der, star of night, Star with roy-al beau-ty bright, West-ward lead-ing

still pro - ceed - ing, Guide us to Thy per - fect light.

Melchior ~

Born a King on Bethlehem's plain,
Gold I bring, to crown Him again,
King for ever, ceasing never,
Over us all to reign.

Caspar ~

Frankincense to offer have I;
Incense owns a Deity nigh,
Prayer and praising, all men raising,
Worship him, God most high.

Balthazar ~

Myrrh is mine, its bitter perfume
Breathes a life of gathering gloom;
Sorrowing, sighing, bleeding, dying,
Sealed in the stone ~ cold tomb.

All ~

Glorious now behold him arise,
King and God and sacrifice.
Alleluia, Alleluia,
Earth to the heavens replies.

J. H. HOPKINS, JR.

33

THE JOURNEY OF THE MAGI

"A cold coming we had of it,
Just the worst time of the year
For a journey, and such a long journey:
The ways deep and the weather sharp,
The very dead of winter."
And the camels galled, sorefooted, refractory,
Lying down in the melting snow.
There were times we regretted
The summer palaces on slopes, the terraces,
And the silken girls bringing sherbet.
Then the camel men cursing and grumbling
And running away, and wanting their liquor and women,
And the night-fires going out, and the lack of shelters,
And the cities hostile and the towns unfriendly
And the villages dirty and charging high prices:
A hard time we had of it.
At the end we preferred to travel all night,

Sleeping in snatches,
With the voices singing in our ears, saying
That this was all folly.

Then at dawn we came down to a temperate valley,
Wet, below the snow line, smelling of vegetation,
With a running stream, and a water-mill beating the darkness,
And three trees on the low sky.
And an old white horse galloped away in the meadow.
Then we came to a tavern with vine-leaves over the lintel,
Six hands at an open door dicing for pieces of silver,
And feet kicking the empty wine-skins.
But there was no information, so we continued
And arrived at evening, not a moment too soon
Finding the place; it was (you may say) satisfactory.

All this was a long time ago, I remember,
And I would do it again, but set down
This set down
This: were we led all that way for
Birth or Death? There was a Birth, certainly,
We had evidence and no doubt. I had seen birth and death,
But had thought they were different; this Birth was
Hard and bitter agony for us, like Death, our death.
We returned to our places, these Kingdoms,
But no longer at ease here, in the old dispensation,
With an alien people clutching their gods.
I should be glad of another death.

T. S. ELIOT

In the Bleak Mid-winter

CRANHAM

Gustav Holst

In the bleak mid-winter
Frosty winds made moan,
Earth stood hard as iron,
Water like a stone;
Snow had fallen, snow on snow,
Snow on snow,
In the bleak mid-winter,
Long ago

2. Our God, heaven cannot hold him
Nor earth sustain;
Heaven and earth shall flee away
When he comes to reign:
In the bleak mid-winter
A stable-place sufficed
The Lord God Almighty,
Jesus Christ.

3. Enough for him, whom cherubim
Worship night and day,
A breastful of milk,
And a mangerful of hay;
Enough for him, whom angels
Fall down before,
The ox and ass and camel
Which adore.

4. Angels and archangels
May have gathered there,
Cherubim and seraphim
Thronged the air:
But only his mother
In her maiden bliss
Worshipped the Belovèd
With a kiss.

5. What can I give him,
Poor as I am?
If I were a shepherd
I would bring a lamb;
If I were a wise man
I would do my part;
Yet what I can I give him —
Give my heart.

Christina Rossetti

In moderate time

1. In the bleak mid ~ win ~ ter Frost ~ y wind made moan, — Earth stood hard as ir ~ on, Wa ~ ter like a stone; Snow had fall ~ en, snow on snow, Snow — on — snow, In the bleak mid ~ win ~ ter, Long — a ~ go

CHRISTMAS

ALL after pleasures as I rid one day,
My horse and I, both tir'd, bodie and minde,
With full crie of affections, quite astray;
I took up in the next inne I could finde.

There when I came, whom found I but my deare,
My dearest Lord, expecting till the grief
Of pleasures brought me to him, readie there
To be all passengers most sweet relief?

O Thou whose glorious, yet contracted light,
Wrapt in nights mantle, stole into a manger;
Since my dark soul and brutish is thy right,
To man of all beasts be not thou a stranger:

Furnish and deck my soul, that thou may'st have
A better lodging, than a rack, or grave.

38

The shepherds sing; and shall I silent be?
My God, no hymne for thee?
My soul's a shepherd too: a flock it feeds
Of thoughts, and words, and deeds.
The pasture is thy word; the streams, thy grace
Enriching all the place.
Shepherd and flock shall sing, and all my powers
Out-sing the day light houres.
Then we will chide the sunne for letting night
Take up his place and right:

We sing one common Lord; wherefore he should
Himself the candle hold.
I will go searching, till I finde a sunne
Shall stay, till we have done;
A willing shiner that shall shine as gladly,
As frost-nip sunnes look sadly.
Then we will sing, and shine all our own day,
And one another pay:
His beams shall cheer my breast, and both so twine,
Till ev'n his beams sing, and my musick shine.

GEORGE HERBERT

39

HYMN ON THE MORNING OF CHRIST'S NATIVITY

Ring out, ye crystal spheres—
Once bless our human ears—
(If ye have power to touch our
senses so)
And let your silver chime—
Move in melodious time,
And let the base of Heaven's
deep organ blow;
And with your ninefold harmony
Make up full consort to the angelic
symphony. ...

JOHN MILTON

THE FIRST NOWELL

1 The First Nowell the angel did say, Was to certain poor shepherds in fields as they lay; In fields where they lay keeping their sheep, On a cold winter's night that was so deep

41

REFRAIN (FULL)

f No - well, - No - well, No - well, - No - well, ——

Born is the King — of Is — — ra - el.

BOYS (Unis.)

BOYS (Unis.)

2. They looked up and saw a star
   Shining in the east, beyond them far,
   And to the earth it gave great light,
   And so it continued both day and night.
   Nowell, etc.

MEN (Unis)

3. And by the light of that same star,
   Three wisemen came from country far
   To seek for a King was their intent,
   And to follow the star wherever it went.
   Nowell, etc.

4. This star drew nigh unto the north-west,
   O'er Bethlehem it took its rest,
   And there it did both stop and stay,
   Right over the place where Jesus lay.
       Nowell, etc.

FULL HARMONY

5. Then entered in those wisemen three,
   Fell reverently upon their knee,
   And offered there, in his presence,
   Their gold, and myrrh, and frankincense.
       Nowell, etc.

FULL (Unis.)

6. Then let us all with one accord
   Sing praises to our heavenly Lord,
   That hath made heaven and earth of nought,
   And with His blood mankind has bought.
       Nowell, etc.

Thou whose birth on earth
Angels sang to men,
While the stars made mirth,
Saviour, at thy birth
This day born again.

As this night was bright
With thy cradle-ray,
Very light of light,
Turn the wild world's night
To thy perfect day.

Bid our peace increase
Thou that madest morn,
Bid oppressions cease;
Bid the night be peace
Bid the day be born.

A.C. SWINBURNE.

44

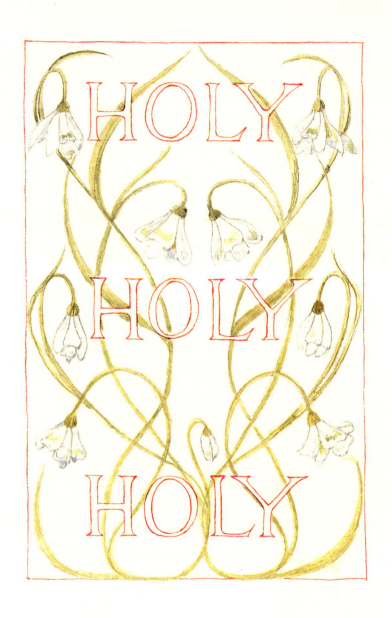

Be merry all,
Be merry all,
With holly dress the festive hall;
Prepare the song,
the feast, the ball,
To welcome merry
Christmas.

W. R. Spencer

Time was
with most of us, when
Christmas Day, encircling all
our limited world like a magic
ring, left nothing out for us to miss
or seek; bound together all our home
enjoyments, affections, and hopes;
grouped everything and everyone
round the Christmas fire, and
made the little picture shining
in our bright young eyes,
complete.

CHARLES DICKENS

47

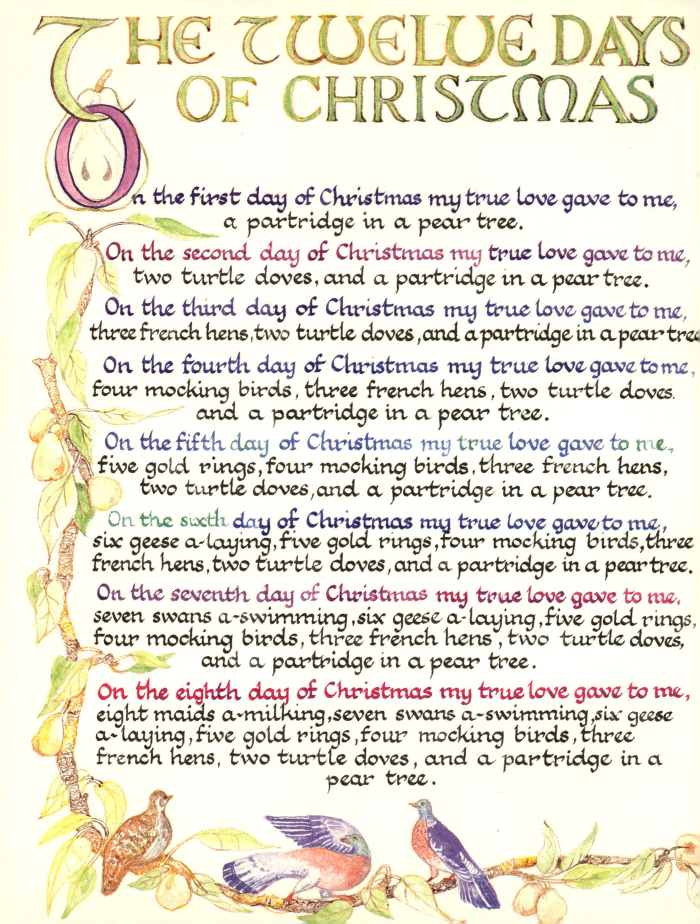

THE TWELVE DAYS OF CHRISTMAS

On the first day of Christmas my true love gave to me,
a partridge in a pear tree.

On the second day of Christmas my true love gave to me,
two turtle doves, and a partridge in a pear tree.

On the third day of Christmas my true love gave to me,
three french hens, two turtle doves, and a partridge in a pear tree.

On the fourth day of Christmas my true love gave to me,
four mocking birds, three french hens, two turtle doves,
and a partridge in a pear tree.

On the fifth day of Christmas my true love gave to me,
five gold rings, four mocking birds, three french hens,
two turtle doves, and a partridge in a pear tree.

On the sixth day of Christmas my true love gave to me,
six geese a-laying, five gold rings, four mocking birds, three
french hens, two turtle doves, and a partridge in a pear tree.

On the seventh day of Christmas my true love gave to me,
seven swans a-swimming, six geese a-laying, five gold rings,
four mocking birds, three french hens, two turtle doves,
and a partridge in a pear tree.

On the eighth day of Christmas my true love gave to me,
eight maids a-milking, seven swans a-swimming, six geese
a-laying, five gold rings, four mocking birds, three
french hens, two turtle doves, and a partridge in a
pear tree.

On the ninth day of Christmas my true love gave to me,
nine ladies waiting, eight maids a-milking, seven swans
a-swimming, six geese a-laying, five gold rings, four
mocking birds, three french hens, two turtle doves,
and a partridge in a pear tree.

On the tenth day of Christmas my true love gave to me,
ten lords a-leaping, nine ladies waiting, eight maids
a-milking, seven swans a-swimming, six geese a-
laying, five gold rings, four mocking birds, three french
hens, two turtle doves, and a partridge in a pear tree.

On the eleventh day of Christmas my true love gave to me,
eleven pipers piping, ten lords a-leaping, nine ladies
waiting, eight maids a-milking, seven swans a-swimming, six geese a-laying, five gold rings, four mocking
birds, three french hens, two turtle doves, and a
partridge in a pear tree.

On the twelfth day of Christmas my true love gave to me,
twelve drummers drumming, eleven pipers piping,
ten lords a-leaping, nine ladies waiting, eight maids
a-milking, seven swans a-swimming, six geese a-
laying, five gold rings, four mocking birds, three
french hens, two turtle doves,
and a partridge in a pear tree.

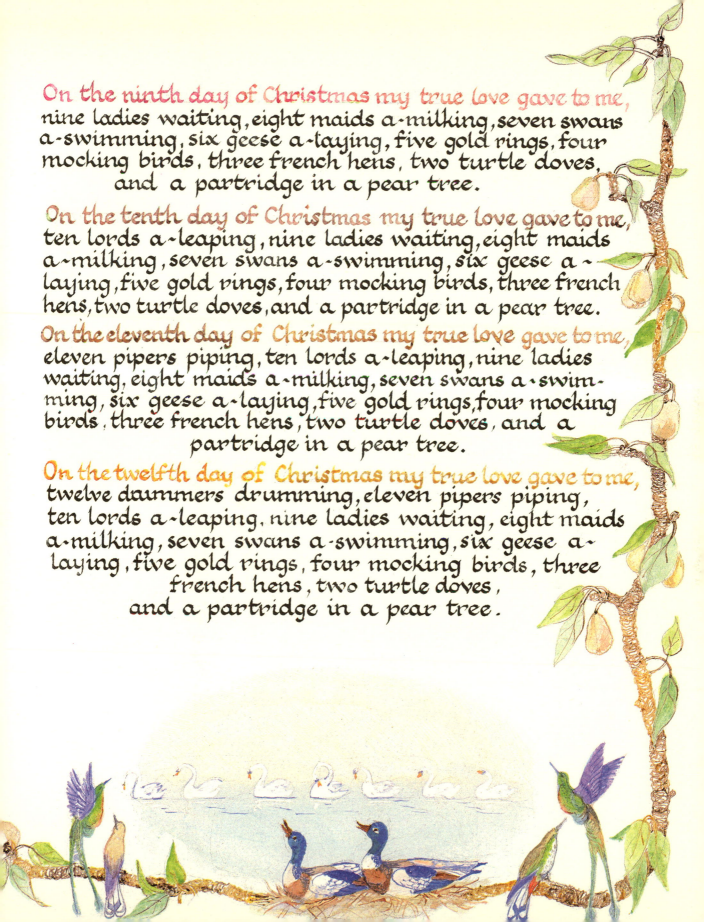

1. On the first day of Christ-mas, my true love gave to me, a par-tridge in a pear tree

2. On the sec-ond day of Christ-mas, my true love gave to me, Two tur-tle doves and a par-tridge in a pear tree.

3. On the third day of Christ-mas, my true love gave to me, Three French hens,

A VISIT

FROM SAINT NICHOLAS

'Twas the night before Christmas, when all through the house
Not a creature was stirring, not even a mouse;
The stockings were hung by the chimney with care,
In hopes that St. Nicholas soon would be there;
The children were nestled all snug in their beds,
While visions of sugar plums danced in their heads;
And mamma in her kerchief, and I in my cap,
Had just settled our brains for a long winter's nap,
When out on the lawn there arose such a clatter,
I sprang from the bed to see what was the matter.
Away to the window I flew like a flash,
Tore open the shutters, and threw up the sash.
The moon on the breast of the new fallen snow

Gave a luster of mid-day to objects below,
When what to my wondering eyes should appear,
But a miniature sleigh and eight tiny reindeer,
With a little old driver, so lively and quick,
I knew in a moment it must be St. Nick.
More rapid than eagles his coursers they came,
And he whistled, and shouted, and called them by name;
Now Dasher! now, Dancer! now, Prancer and Vixen!
On, Comet! on, Cupid! on Dunder and Blitzen!
To the top of the porch! To the top of the wall!
Now dash away! Dash away! Dash away all!"
As dry leaves that before the wild hurricane fly,
When they meet with an obstacle, mount to the sky;
So up to the housetop the coursers they flew,
With the sleigh full of toys, and St. Nicholas, too.
And then in a twinkling, I heard on the roof
The prancing and pawing of each little hoof.
As I drew in my head, and was turning around,
Down the chimney St. Nicholas came with a bound.
He was dressed all in fur from his head to his foot,
And his clothes were all tarnished with ashes and soot;
A bundle of toys he had flung on his back,
And he looked like a peddler just opening his pack.
His eyes ~ how they twinkled! ~ his dimples how merry!
His cheeks were like roses, his nose like a cherry!

His droll little mouth was drawn up like a bow,
And the beard of his chin was as white as the snow;
The stump of a pipe he held tight in his teeth,
And the smoke it encircled his head like a wreath;
He had a broad face and a round little belly,
That shook when he laughed like a bowlful of jelly.
He was chubby and plump, a right jolly old elf,
And I laughed when I saw him in spite of myself;
A wink of his eye and a twist of his head,
Soon gave me to know I had nothing to dread;
He spoke not a word, but went straight to his work,
And filled all the stockings, then turned with a jerk,
And laying his finger aside of his nose,
And giving a nod, up the chimney he rose;
He sprang to his sleigh, to his team gave a whistle,
And away they all flew like the down of a thistle;
But I heard him exclaim ere he drove out of sight,
"Happy Christmas to all, and to all a goodnight!"

CLEMENT MOORE ~

53

was not a good man ~
He had his little ways.
And sometimes no one spoke to him
For days and days and days.
And men who came across him,
When walking in the town,
Gave him a supercilious stare,
Or passed with noses in the air ~
And bad King John stood dumbly there,
Blushing beneath his crown.

King John was not a good man,
And no good friends had he.
He stayed in every afternoon...
But no one came to tea.
And, round about December,
The cards upon his shelf
Which wished him lots of Christmas cheer
And fortune in the coming year,
Were never from his near and dear,
But only from himself.

KING JOHN

was not a good man,
Yet had his hopes and fears.
They'd given him no present now
For years and years and years.
But every year at Christmas,
While minstrels stood about,
Collecting tribute from the young
For all the songs they might have sung,
He stole away upstairs and hung
A hopeful stocking out.

King John was not a good man,
He lived his life aloof;
Alone he thought a message out
While climbing up the roof.
He wrote it down and propped it
Against the chimney stack:
"TO ALL AND SUNDRY – NEAR AND FAR –
F. CHRISTMAS IN PARTICULAR."
And signed it not "Johannes R."
But very humbly "JACK".

"I want some crackers,
And I want some candy;
I think a box of chocolates
Would come in handy;
I don't mind oranges,
I do like nuts!

To all and
sundry – near
and far –
F. CHRISTMAS
in particular

55

And I SHOULD like a pocket-knife
That really cuts.
And, oh! Father Christmas, if you love me at all,
Bring me a big, red india-rubber ball!"

King John was not a good man ~
He wrote this message out,
And gat him to his room again,
Descending by the spout.
And all that night he lay there,
A prey to hopes and fears.
"I think that's him a-coming now,"
(Anxiety bedewed his brow.)
"He'll bring one present, anyhow ~
The first I've had for years."

"Forget about the crackers,
And forget about the candy;
I'm sure a box of chocolates
Would never come in handy;
I don't like oranges,
I don't want nuts,
And I have got a pocket-knife
That almost cuts.
But, oh! Father Christmas, if you love me at all,
Bring me a big, red india-rubber ball."

King John was not a good man ~
Next morning when the sun
Rose up to tell a waiting world
That Christmas had begun,
And people seized their stockings,
And opened them with glee,
And crackers, toys and games appeared,
And lips with sticky sweets were smeared,
King John said grimly: "As I feared,
Nothing again for me!"

'I did want crackers,
And I did want candy;
I know a box of chocolates
Would come in handy;
I do love oranges,
I did want nuts.
I haven't got a pocket-knife ~
Not one that cuts.
And, oh! if Father Christmas had loved me at all,
He would have brought a big, red india-rubber ball!"

King John stood by the window,
And frowned to see below
The happy bands of boys and girls
All playing in the snow.
A while he stood there watching,
And envying them all . . .
When through the window big and red
There hurtled by his royal head,
And bounced and fell upon the bed,
An india-rubber ball!

AND OH, FATHER CHRISTMAS,
MY BLESSINGS ON YOU FALL
FOR BRINGING HIM A BIG, RED,
INDIA-RUBBER
BALL!

A. A. MILNE

GOOD KING WENCESLAS

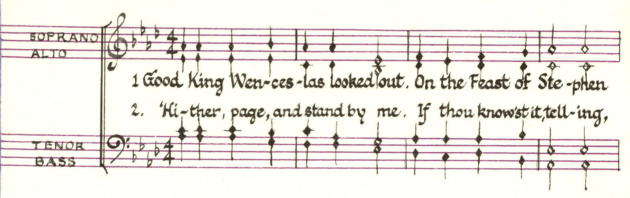

SOPRANO
ALTO

1 Good King Wen-ces-las looked out. On the Feast of Ste-phen

2. 'Hi-ther, page, and stand by me. If thou know'st it, tell-ing,

TENOR
BASS

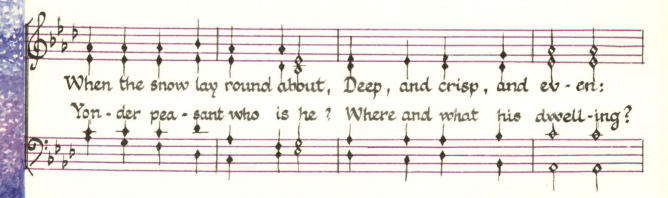

When the snow lay round about, Deep, and crisp, and ev-en:

Yon-der pea-sant who is he? Where and what his dwell-ing?

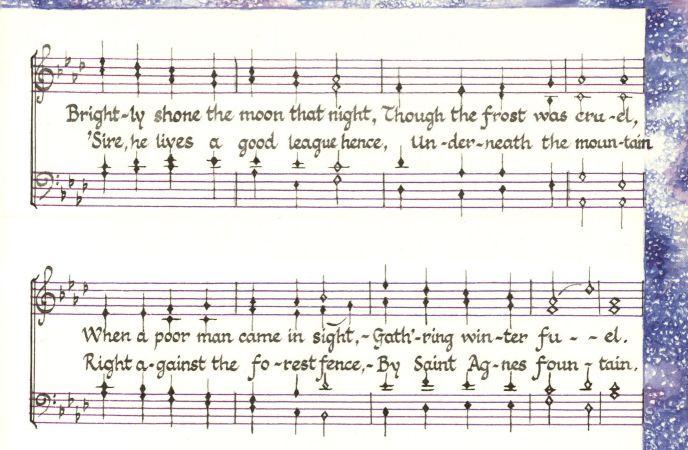

Brightly shone the moon that night, Though the frost was cruel,
'Sire, he lives a good league hence, Underneath the mountain

When a poor man came in sight, ~ Gath'ring winter fu ~ ~ el.
Right against the fo ~ rest fence, ~ By Saint Agnes foun ~ tain.

'Bring me bread and bring me wine.
Bring me pine ~ logs hither;
Thou and I shall see him dine,
When we bear them thither.'
Page and monarch, forth they went.
Forth they went together;
Through the rude wind's wild lament
And the bitter weather.

'Sire, the night is darker now,
And the wind blows stronger;
Fails my heart, I know not how;
I can go no longer.'
'Mark my footsteps, good my page;
Tread thou in them boldly;
Thou shalt find the winter's rage
Freeze thy blood less coldly.

In his master's steps he trod,
Where the snow lay dinted;
Heat was in the very sod
Which the saint had printed,
Therefore, Christian men, be sure,
Wealth or rank possessing,
Ye who now will bless the poor,
Shall yourselves find blessing.

JOHN MASON NEALE

62

 **IS** the season for
kindling the fire of
hospitality in the hall,
the genial fire of
charity in the heart.

Washington Irving

63

Conversation about Christmas

Small Boy. Years and years ago, when you were a boy......

Self ~ When there were wolves in Wales, and birds the colour of red~flannel petticoats whisked past the harp-shaped hills, when we sang and wallowed all night and day in caves that smelt like Sunday afternoons in damp front farmhouse parlours, and chased, with the jawbones of deacons, the English and the bears —— ...

Small Boy. When you were a boy, what was Christmas like?

Self ~ It snowed.

Small Boy. It snowed last year, too. I made a snowman and my brother knocked it down and I knocked my brother down and then we had tea.

Self ~ But that was not the same snow. Our snow was not only shaken in whitewash buckets down the sky, I think it came shawling out of the ground and swam and drifted out of the arms and hands and bodies of the trees; snow grew over~night on the roofs of the houses like a pure and grandfather moss, minutely ivied the walls, and settled on the postman,

64

opening the gate, like a dumb, numb thunderstorm of white torn
Christmas cards.

Small Boy — Were there postmen, then, too?

Self — With sprinkling eyes and wind-cherried noses, on spread,
frozen feet they crunched up to the doors and mittened
on them manfully. But all that the children could hear was a
ringing of bells.

Small Boy — You mean that the postman went rat-a-tat-tat and
the doors rang?

Self — The bells that the children could hear were inside
them.

Small Boy — I only hear thunder sometimes, never bells.

Self — There were church bells, too.

Small Boy — Inside them?

Self — No, no, no, in the bat-black, snow-white belfries,
tugged by bishops and storks. And they rang their tidings over
the bandaged town, over the frozen foam of the powder and
ice-cream hills, over the crackling sea. It seemed that all the
churches boomed, for joy, under my window; and the weather-
cocks crew for Christmas, on our fence.

Small Boy — Get back to the postmen.

Self – They were just ordinary postmen, fond of walking, and dogs, and Christmas, and the snow. They knocked on the doors with blue knuckles —

Small Boy Ours has got a black knocker —

Self – And then they stood on the white welcome mat in the little, drifted porches, and clapped their hands together, and huffed and puffed, making ghosts with their breath, and jogged from foot to foot like small boys wanting to go out.

Small Boy And then the presents?

Self – And then the Presents, after the Christmas Box. And the cold postman, with a rose on his button~nose, tingled down the teatray~slithered run of the chilly glinting hill. He went in his ice~bound boots like a man on fishmonger's slabs. He wagged his bag like a frozen camel's hump, dizzily turned the corner on one foot, and, by God, he was gone.

Small Boy Get back to the Presents.

Self – There were the Useful Presents: engulfing mufflers of the old coach days, and mittens made for giant sloths; zebra scarves of a substance like silky gum that could be tug~o~warred down to the goloshes; blinding tam~o~shanters like patchwork tea~cosies, and bunnyscutted busbies and balaclavas for victims of headshrinking tribes; from aunts who always wore wool~next~to~the~skin, there were moustached and rasping vests that made you wonder why the aunties

66

had any skin left at all; and once I had a little crocheted nose-
bag from an aunt now, alas, no longer whinnying with us.
And pictureless books in which small boys, though warned,
with quotations, not to, would skate on Farmer Garge's pond,
and did, and drowned; and books that told me everything
about the wasp, except why.

Small Boy **Get** on to the Useless Presents.

Self ~ **On** Christmas Eve I hung at the foot of my bed
Bessie Bunter's black stocking, and always, I said, I would
stay awake all the moonlit, snowlit night to hear the roof ~
alighting reindeer and see the hollied boot descend through
soot. But soon the sand of the snow drifted into my eyes, and,
though I stared towards the fireplace and around the flicker-
ing room where the black sack-like stocking hung, I was a-
sleep before the chimney trembled and the room was red and
white with Christmas. But in the morning, though no snow
melted on the bedroom floor, the stocking bulged and brimmed:
press it, it squeaked like a mouse-in-a-box; it smelt of
tangerine; a furry arm lolled over, like the arm of a kangaroo
out of its mother's belly; squeeze it hard in the middle, and
something squelched; squeeze it again ~ squelch again. Look out
of the frost~scribbled window; on the great loneliness of the
small hill, a blackbird was silent in the snow.

Small Boy **Were** there any sweets?

Self ~ **Of** course there were sweets. It was the marsh-
mallows that squelched. Hardboileds, toffee, fudge and allsorts,
crunches, cracknels, humbugs, glaciers, and marzipan and

67

butterwelsh for the Welsh. And troops of bright tin soldiers who, if they would not fight, could always run. And Snakes-and-Families and Happy Ladders. And Easy Hobbi-Games for Little Engineers, complete with Instructions. Oh, easy for Leonardo! And a whistle to make the dogs bark to wake up the old man next door to make him beat on the wall with his stick to shake our picture off the wall. And a packet of cigarettes: you put one in your mouth and you stood at the corner of the street and you waited for hours, in vain, for an old lady to scold you for smoking a cigarette and then, with a smirk, you ate it. And, last of all, in the toe of the stocking, sixpence like a silver corn. And then downstairs for breakfast under the balloons!

Small Boy ~ Were there Uncles, like in our house?

Self ~ There are always Uncles at Christmas. The same Uncles. And on Christmas mornings, with dog-disturbing whistles and sugar fags, I would scour the swathed town for news of the little world, and find always a dead bird by the white bank or by the deserted swings: perhaps a robin, all but one of his fires out, and that fire still burning on his breast. Men and women wading and scooping back from church or chapel, with taproom noses and wind-smacked cheeks, all albinos, huddled their stiff black jarring feathers against the irreligious snow. Mistletoe hung from the gas in all the front parlours: there was sherry and walnuts and bottled beer and crackers by the dessert-spoons; and cats in their fur-abouts watched the fires; and the high-heaped fires crackled and spat, all ready for the chestnuts and the mulling pokers. Some few large men sat in the front parlours without their collars, Uncles almost certainly, trying their new cigars, holding them out judiciously at arms-length, returning them to their mouths, coughing, then holding them out again as though waiting for the explosion; and some few small aunts, not wanted in the kitchen, nor anywhere else for that matter, sat on the edges of their chairs, poised and brittle, afraid to speak, like faded cups and saucers. Not many those mornings trod the piling streets: an old man always, fawn-bowlered, yellow-gloved, and, at this time of year, with spats of snow, would take his constitutional to the white bowling-green, and back, as he would take it wet or fine on Christmas Day or Doomsday; sometimes two hale young men, with big pipes blazing, no overcoats, and windblown scarves, would trudge, unspeaking, down to the forlorn sea, to work up an appetite, to blow away the fumes, who knows, to walk into the waves until nothing of them was left but the two curling smoke clouds of their inextinguishable briars.

Small Boy.

Self.

Why didn't you go home for Christmas dinner?

Oh, but I did, I always did. I would be slap-dashing home, the gravy smell of the dinners of others, the bird smell, the brandy, the pudding and mince, weaving up my nostrils, when out of a snow-clogged side-lane would come a boy the spit of myself, with a pink-tipped cigarette and the violet past of a black eye, cocky as a bullfinch, leering all to himself. I hated him on sight and sound, and— would be about to put my dog-whistle to my lips and blow him off the face of Christmas when suddenly he, with a violet wink, put his whistle to his lips and blew so stridently, so high, so exquisitely loud, that gobbling faces, their cheeks bulged with goose, would press against their tinselled windows, the whole length of the white echoing street.

Small Boy – **W**hat did you have for Dinner?

Self – **T**urkey, and blazing pudding.

Small Boy – **W**as it nice?

Self – **I**t was not made on earth.

Small Boy – **W**hat did you do after dinner?

Self – **T**he Uncles sat in front of the fire, took off their collars, loosened all buttons, put their large moist hands over their watch-chains, groaned a little, and slept. Mothers, aunts, and sisters scuttled to and fro, bearing tureens. The dog was sick. Auntie Beattie had to have three aspirins, but Auntie Hannah, who liked port, stood in the middle of the snowbound back-yard, singing like a big-bosomed thrush. I would blow up balloons to see how big they would blow up to; and, when they burst, which they all did, the Uncles jumped and rumbled. In the rich and heavy afternoon, the Uncles breathing like dolphins and the snow descending, I would sit in the front room, among festoons and Chinese lanterns, and nibble at dates, and try to make a model man-o'-war, following the Instructions for Little Engineers, and produce what might be mistaken for a sea-going tram. And then, at Christmas tea, the recovered Uncles would be jolly over their mince-pies; and the great iced cake loomed in the centre of the table like a marble grave. Auntie Hannah laced her tea with rum, because it was only once a year. And in the evening there was Music. An Uncle played the fiddle, a cousin sang 'Cherry Ripe' and another

70

uncle sang 'Drake's Drum'. It was very warm in the little house. Auntie Hannah, who had got on to the parsnip wine, sang a song about Rejected Love, and Bleeding Hearts, and Death, and then another in which she said that her Heart was like a Bird's Nest; and then everybody laughed again, and then I went to bed. Looking through my bedroom window, out into the moonlight and the flying, unending, smoke-coloured snow, I could see the lights in the windows of all the other houses on our hill, and hear the music rising from them up the long, steadily falling night. I turned the gas down, I got into bed. I said some words to the close and holy darkness, and then I slept.

Small Boy - **B**ut it all sounds like an ordinary Christmas.

Self - **I**t was.

Small Boy - **B**ut Christmas when you were a boy wasn't any different to Christmas now.

Self - **I**t was, it was.

Small Boy - **W**hy was Christmas different then?

Self - **I** mustn't tell you.

Small Boy - **W**hy mustn't you tell me? Why is Christmas different for me?

Self - **I** mustn't tell you.

71

Small Boy - Why can't Christmas be the same for me as it was for you when you were a boy?

Self ~ I musn't tell you. I musn't tell you because it is Christmas now.

Dylan Thomas

QUESTIONING FACES

The winter owl banked just in time to pass
And save herself from breaking window glass.
And her wings straining suddenly aspread
Caught color from the last of evening red
In a display of underdown and quill
To glassed-in children at the window-sill.

ROBERT FROST

THE LITTLE MATCH GIRL

It was bitterly cold, snow was falling and darkness was gathering, for it was the last evening of the old year – it was New Year's Eve.

In the cold and gloom a poor little girl walked, bareheaded and barefoot, through the streets. She had been wearing slippers, it is true, when she left home, but what good were they? They had been her mother's, so you can imagine how big they were. The little girl had lost them as she ran across the street to escape from two carriages that were being driven terribly fast. One slipper could not be found, and a boy had run off with the other, saying that would come in very handy as a cradle some day when he had children of his own.

So the little girl walked about the streets on her naked feet, which were red and blue with the cold. In her old apron she carried a great many matches, and she had a packet of them in her hand as well. Nobody had bought any from her, and no one had given her a single penny all day. She crept along, shivering and hungry, the picture of misery, poor little thing!

The snowflakes fell on her long golden hair which curled so prettily about her neck, but she did not think of her appearance now. Lights were shining in every window, and their was a glorious smell of roast goose in the street, for this was New Year's Eve, and she could not think of anything else.

She huddled down in a heap in a corner formed by two houses, one of which projected further out into the street than the other, but though she tucked her little legs up under her she felt colder and colder. She did not dare go home, for she had sold no matches and earned not a single penny. Her father would be sure to beat her, and besides it was so cold at home, for they had nothing but the roof above them and the wind whistled through that, even though the largest cracks were stuffed with straw and rags. Her thin hands were almost numb with cold. If only she dared pull just one small match from the packet, strike it on the wall and warm her fingers!

She pulled one out ~ scr-r-ratch! ~ how it spluttered and burnt! It had a warm, bright flame like a tiny candle when she held her hand over it - but what a strange light! It seemed to the little girl as if she were sitting in front of a great iron stove with polished brass knobs and brass ornaments. The fire burnt so beautifully and gave out such a lovely warmth. Oh, how wonderful that was! The child had already stretched her feet to warm them, too, when - out went the flame, the stove vanished and there she sat with the burnt match in her hand.

She struck another - it burnt clearly and, where the light fell upon the wall, the bricks became transparent, like gauze. She could see right into the room, where a shining white cloth was spread on the table. It was covered with beautiful china and in the centre of it stood a roast goose, stuffed with prunes and apples, steaming deliciously. And what was even more wonderful was that the goose hopped down from the dish, waddled across the floor with carving knife and fork in its back, waddled straight up to the poor child! Then - out went the match, and nothing could be seen but the thick, cold wall.

She struck another match, and suddenly she was sitting under the most beautiful Christmas tree. It was much larger and much lovelier than the one she had seen last year through the glass doors of the rich merchant's house. A thousand candles lit up the green branches, and gaily coloured balls like those in the shop windows looked down upon her. The little girl reached forward with both hands ~ then, out went the match. The many candles on the Christmas tree rose higher and higher through the air, and she saw that they had now turned into bright stars. One of them fell, streaking the sky with light.

"Now someone is dying," said the little girl, for her old grandmother, the only one who had ever been good to her but who was now dead, had said, "Whenever a star falls, a soul goes up to God."

She struck another match on the wall. Once more there was light, and in the glow stood her old grandmother, oh, so bright and shining, and looking so gentle, kind and loving. "Granny!" cried the little girl. "Oh, take me with you! I know you will disappear when the match is burnt out; you will vanish like the warm stove, the lovely roast goose and the great glorious Christmas tree!"

Then she quickly struck all the rest of the matches she had in the packet, for she did so want to keep her grandmother with her.

The matches flared up with such a blaze that it was brighter than broad daylight, and her old grandmother had never seemed so beautiful or so stately before. She took the little girl in her arms and flew with her high up, oh, so high, towards glory and joy! Now they knew neither cold nor hunger nor fear, for they were both with God.

But in the cold dawn, in the corner formed by the two houses, sat the little girl with rosy cheeks and smiling lips, dead — frozen to death on the last evening of the old year. The dawn of the new year rose on the huddled figure of the girl. She was still holding the matches, and half a packet had been burnt.

"She was evidently trying to warm herself," people said. But no one knew what beautiful visions she had seen and in what a blaze of glory she had entered with her dear old grandmother into the heavenly joy and gladness of a new year.

HANS CHRISTIAN ANDERSEN

YULETIDE IN A YOUNGER WORLD

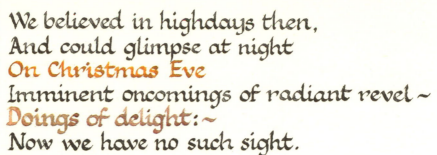

We believed in highdays then,
And could glimpse at night
On Christmas Eve
Imminent oncomings of radiant revel ~
Doings of delight: ~
Now we have no such sight.

We had eyes for phantoms then,
And at bridge or stile
On Christmas Eve
Clear beheld those countless ones who had crossed it
Cross again in file: ~
Such has ceased longwhile!

We liked divination then,
And, as they homeward wound
On Christmas Eve
We could read men's dreams within them spinning
Even as wheels spin round: ~
Now we are blinker ~ bound.

We heard still small voices then,
And, in the dim serene
On Christmas Eve,
Caught the far ~ times tones of fire ~ filled prophets
Long on earth unseen...
~ Can such ever have been?

Thomas Hardy.

79

A CAROL FOR CHILDREN

God rest you, merry Innocents,
Let nothing you dismay,
Let nothing wound an eager heart
Upon this Christmas day.

Yours be the genial holly wreaths,
The stockings and the tree;
An aged world to you bequeaths
Its own forgotten glee.

Soon, soon enough come crueler gifts,
The anger and the tears;
Between you now there sparsely drifts
A handful yet of years.

Oh, dimly, dimly glows the star
Through the electric throng;
The bidding in temple and bazaar
Drowns out the silver song.

The ancient altars smoke afresh,
The ancient idols stir;
Faint in the reek of burning flesh
Sink frankincense and myrrh.

Gaspar, Balthazar, Melchior!
Where are your offerings now?
What greetings to the Prince of War,
His darkly branded brow?

Two ultimate laws alone we know,
The ledger and the sword —
So far away, so long ago,
We lost the infant Lord.

Only the children clasp his hand;
His voice speaks low to them.
And still for them the shining band
Wings over Bethlehem.

God rest you, merry Innocents,
While innocence endures.
A sweeter Christmas than we to ours
May **you** bequeath to yours.

OGDEN NASH

81

CHRISTMAS

The bells of waiting Advent ring,
The tortoise stove is lit again
And lamp-oil light across the night
Has caught the streaks of winter rain
In many a stained glass window sheen
From Crimson Lake to Hooker's Green.

The holly in the windy hedge
And round the Manor House the yew
Will soon be stripped to deck the ledge,
The altar, font and arch and pew,
So that the villagers can say
"The church looks nice" on Christmas Day.

Provincial public houses blaze
And Corporation tramcars clang,
On lighted tenements I gaze
Where paper decorations hang,
And bunting in the red Town Hall
Says "Merry Christmas to you all."

And London shops on Christmas Eve
Are strung with silver bells and flowers
As hurrying clerks the City leave
To pigeon-haunted classic towers,
And marbled clouds go scudding by
The many-steepled London sky.

BY JOHN BETJEMAN

And girls in slacks remember Dad,
And oafish louts remember Mum,
And sleepless children's hearts are glad,
And Christmas-morning bells say "Come!"
Even to shining ones who dwell
Safe in the Dorchester Hotel.

And is it true? And is it true,
This most tremendous tale of all,
Seen in a stained-glass window's hue,
A Baby in an ox's stall?
The Maker of the stars and sea
Become a Child on earth for me.

And is it true? For if it is,
No loving fingers tying strings
Around those tissued fripperies,
The sweet and silly Christmas things,
Bath salts and inexpensive scent,
And hideous tie so kindly meant,

No love that in a family dwells,
No carolling in frosty air,
Nor all the steeple-shaking bells
Can with this single Truth compare ~
That God was man in Palestine
And lives to-day in Bread and Wine.

83

DECEMBER

Glad Christmas and a happy year
To every morning passer-by;
Milkmaids their Christmas journeys go,
Accompanied by favoured swain;
And children pace the crumping snow,
To taste their granny's cake again.

The shepherd, now no more afraid,
Since custom doth the chance bestow
Starts up to kiss the giggling maid
Beneath the branch of mistletoe
That neath each cottage beam is seen,
With pearl like berries shining gay,
The shadow still of what hath been,
Which fashion yearly fades away.

The singing waits, a merry throng,
At early morn, with simple skill,
Yet imitate the angel's song,
And chant their christmas ditty still;
And, mid the storm that dies and swells
By fits, in hummings softly steals
The music of the village bells,
Ringing round their merry peals.

84

BY JOHN CLARE

When this is past, a merry crew,
Bedeck'd in masks and ribbons gay,
The morris dance, their sports renew,
And act their winter evening play.
The clown turned king, for penny praise,
Storms with the actor's strut and swell;
And Harlequin, a laugh to raise,
Wears his hunchback and tinkling bell

And oft for pence and spicy ale,
With winter nosegays pinned before,
The wassail-singer tells her tale,
And drawls her Christmas carols o'er.
While 'prentice boy, with ruddy face,
And rime bepowdered, dancing locks,
From door to door with happy pace,
Runs round to claim his 'Christmas box.'

Old customs! Oh! I love the sound,
However simple they may be;
What e'er with time hath sanction found,
Is welcome and is dear to me.

Shortly after ten o'clock the singing-boys arrived and preparations were made for the start. The older men and musicians wore thick coats, with stiff perpendicular collars, and coloured handkerchiefs wound round and round the neck till the end came to hand, over all which they just showed their ears and noses, like people looking over a wall. The remainder, stalwart ruddy men and boys, were dressed mainly in snow-white smock-frocks, embroidered upon the shoulders and breasts in ornamental forms of hearts, diamonds and zig-zags. The cider-mug was emptied for the ninth time, the music-books were arranged, and the pieces finally decided upon. The boys in the meantime put the old horn-lanterns in order, cut candles into short lengths to fit the lanterns; and, a thin fleece of snow having fallen since the early part of the evening, those who had no leggings went to the stable and wound wisps of hay round their ankles to keep the insidious flakes from the interior of their boots.

THOMAS HARDY

And then, when the night has turned twelve the air brings
From dim distance, a rhythm of voices and strings:
'Tis the quire, just afoot on their yearly rounds,
To rouse by worn carols each house in their bounds.

THE BOAR'S HEAD CAROL

A student of The Queen's College, attacked by a wild boar on Christmas Day, choked the animal by stuffing a copy of Aristotle down its throat. He then cut off the head (to retrieve his book) and carried it to the College's High Table, where the feast is celebrated each year

MALE VOICE SOLO

1. The boar's head in hand bear I, Be-
2. The boar's head, as I un – der – stand, Is the

decked with bays and rose – ma – ry; And I
rar – est dish in all the land When

pray you, my mas – ters, be mer – ry, Quot
thus be – decked with a gay gar – land, Let

es – tis in con – vi – vi – o:
us ser – vi – re can – ti – co:

The boar's head in hand bear I,
Bedecked with bays and rosemary;
And I pray you, my masters, be merry,
  Quot estis in convivio:
  Caput apri defero,
  Reddens laudes Domino.

The boar's head, as I understand,
Is the rarest dish in all the land
When thus bedecked with a gay garland,
  Let us servire cantico:

Our steward hath provided this
In honour of the king of bliss,
Which on this day to be servéd is,
  In Regimensi atrio:

          Oxford

The Grocers! oh the Grocers! nearly closed, with perhaps two shutters down, or one; but through those gaps such glimpses! It was not alone that the scales descending on the counter made a merry sound, or that the twine and roller parted company so briskly, or that the canisters were rattled up and down like juggling tricks, or even that the blended scents of tea and coffee were so grateful to the nose, or even that the raisins were so plentiful and rare, the almonds so extremely white, the sticks of cinnamon so long and straight, the other spices so delicious, the candied fruits so caked and spotted with molten sugar as to make the coldest lookers-on feel faint and subsequently bilious. Nor was it that that the figs were moist and pulpy, or that the French plums blushed in modest tartness from their highly-decorated boxes, or that everything was good to eat and in its Christmas dress...

NUTS

M. JONES & C°

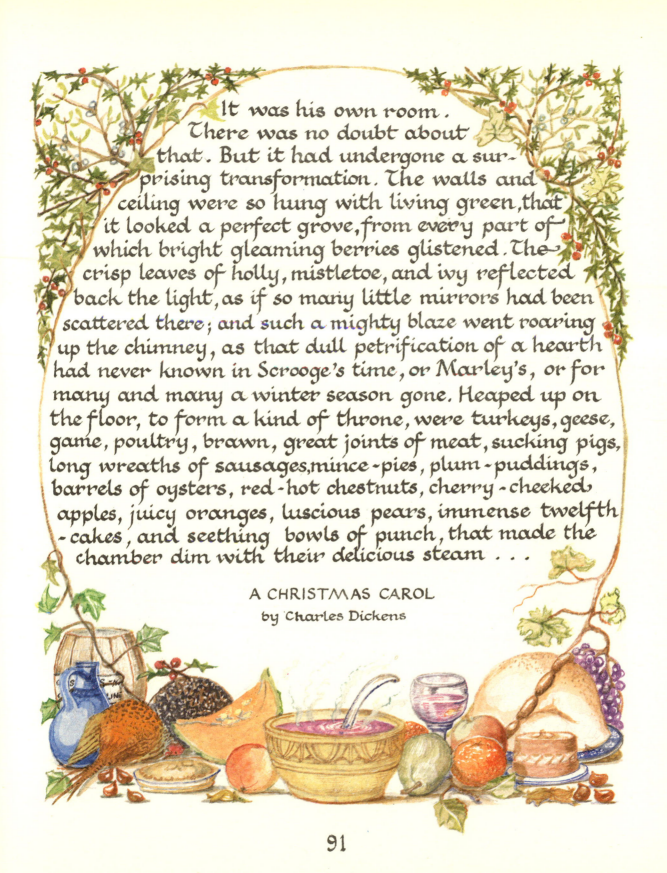

It was his own room.
There was no doubt about
that. But it had undergone a sur-
prising transformation. The walls and
ceiling were so hung with living green, that
it looked a perfect grove, from every part of
which bright gleaming berries glistened. The
crisp leaves of holly, mistletoe, and ivy reflected
back the light, as if so many little mirrors had been
scattered there; and such a mighty blaze went roaring
up the chimney, as that dull petrification of a hearth
had never known in Scrooge's time, or Marley's, or for
many and many a winter season gone. Heaped up on
the floor, to form a kind of throne, were turkeys, geese,
game, poultry, brawn, great joints of meat, sucking pigs,
long wreaths of sausages, mince-pies, plum-puddings,
barrels of oysters, red-hot chestnuts, cherry-cheeked
apples, juicy oranges, luscious pears, immense twelfth
-cakes, and seething bowls of punch, that made the
chamber dim with their delicious steam . . .

A CHRISTMAS CAROL
by Charles Dickens

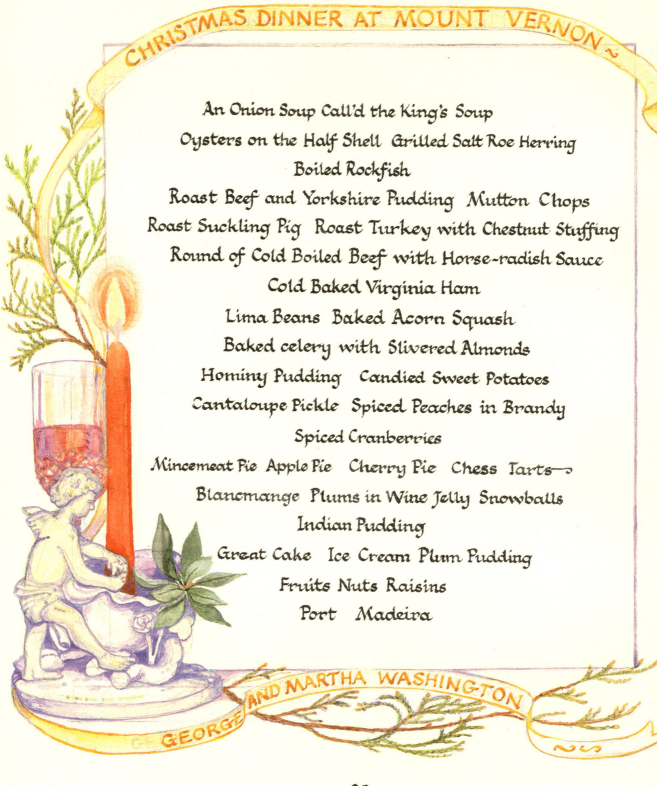

CHRISTMAS DINNER AT MOUNT VERNON ~

An Onion Soup Call'd the King's Soup

Oysters on the Half Shell Grilled Salt Roe Herring

Boiled Rockfish

Roast Beef and Yorkshire Pudding Mutton Chops

Roast Suckling Pig Roast Turkey with Chestnut Stuffing

Round of Cold Boiled Beef with Horse-radish Sauce

Cold Baked Virginia Ham

Lima Beans Baked Acorn Squash

Baked celery with Slivered Almonds

Hominy Pudding   Candied Sweet Potatoes

Cantaloupe Pickle Spiced Peaches in Brandy

Spiced Cranberries

Mincemeat Pie Apple Pie   Cherry Pie   Chess Tarts

Blancmange Plums in Wine Jelly Snowballs

Indian Pudding

Great Cake   Ice Cream Plum Pudding

Fruits Nuts Raisins

Port   Madeira

GEORGE AND MARTHA WASHINGTON

92

CHRISTMAS PLUM-PUDDING

INGREDIENTS ~ 1½ lb. of raisins, ½ lb of currants, ¾ lb of breadcrumbs, ½ lb of mixed peel, ¾ lb of suet, 8 eggs, 1 wineglassful of brandy.

MODE ~ Stone and cut the raisons in halves, but do not chop them; wash, pick and dry the currants, and mince the suet finely; cut the candied peel into thin slices, and grate down the bread into fine crumbs.

When all these dry ingredients are prepared, mix them well together; then moisten the mixture with the eggs, which should be well beaten, and the brandy; stir well, that every thing may be very thoroughly blended, and press the pudding into a buttered mould; tie it down tightly with a floured cloth, and boil for five or six hours. It may be boiled in a cloth without a mould, and will require the same time allowed for cooking.

As Christmas puddings are usually made a few days before they are required for table, when the pudding is taken out of the pot, hang it up immediately, and put a plate or saucer underneath to catch the water that may drain from it. The day it is to be eaten, plunge it into boiling water, and keep it boiling for at least two hours; then turn it out of the mould, and serve with brandy sauce. On Christmas day a sprig of holly is usually placed in the middle of the pudding and about a wineglassful of brandy poured round it, which at the moment of serving, is lighted and the pudding thus brought to the table encircled in flame.

MRS. BEETON

Last of flowers in tufts around
Shines the gorse's golden bloom:
Milk-white lichens clothe the ground
'Mid the flowerless heath and broom:
Bright are holly-berries, seen
Red, through leaves of glossy green.

Brightly, as on rocks they leap,
Shine the sea-waves, white with spray:
Brightly, in the dingles deep,
Gleams the river's foaming way;
Brightly through the distance show
Mountain summits clothed in snow.

Brightly, where the torrents bound,
Shines the frozen colonnade,
Which the black rocks, dripping round,
And the flying spray have made:
Bright the ice-drops on the ash
Leaning o'er the cataract's dash.

94

Bright the hearth, where feast and song
Crown the warrior's hour of peace,
While the snow-storm drives along,
Bidding war's worse tempest cease;
Bright the hearth-flame, flashing clear
On the up-hung shield and spear.

Bright the torchlight of the hall
When the wintry night-winds blow;
Brightest when its splendours fall
On the mead-cup's sparkling flow:
While the maiden's smile of light
Makes the brightness trebly bright.

Close the portals; pile the hearth;
Strike the harp; the feast pursue;
Brim the horns: fire, music, mirth,
Mead and love, are winter's due.
Spring to purple conflict calls
Swords that shine on winter's walls.

The Brilliancies of Winter
                    Thomas Love Peacock

95

LONDON SNOW

When men were all asleep the snow came flying,
In large white flakes falling on the city brown,
Stealthily and perpetually settling and loosely lying,
Hushing the latest traffic of the drowsy town;
Deadening, muffling, stifling its murmurs failing;
Lazily and incessantly floating down and down:
Silently sifting and veiling road, roof and railing;
Hiding difference, making unevenness even,
Into angles and crevices softly drifting and sailing.
All night it fell, and when full inches seven
It lay in the depth of its uncompacted lightness,
The clouds blew off from a high and frosty heaven;
And all woke earlier for the unaccustomed brightness
Of the winter dawning, the strange unheavenly glare:
The eye marvelled ~ marvelled at the dazzling whiteness;

The ear hearkened to the stillness of the solemn air;
No sound of wheel rumbling nor of foot falling,
And the busy morning cries came thin and spare.
Then boys I heard, as they went to school, calling,
They gathered up the crystal manna to freeze
Their tongues with tasting, their hands with snow-
                                    balling;
Or rioted in a drift, plunging up to the knees;
Or peering up from under the white-mossed wonder,
'O look at the trees!' they cried, 'O look at the trees!'
With lessened load a few carts creak and blunder,
Following along the white deserted way,
A country company long dispersed asunder:
When now already the sun, in pale display
Standing by Paul's high dome, spread forth below
His sparkling beams, and awoke the stir of the day.
For now doors open, and war is waged with the
                                    snow;
And trains of sombre men, past tale of number,
Tread long brown paths, as toward their toil they go:
But even for them awhile no cares encumber
Their minds diverted; the daily word is unspoken,
The daily thoughts of labour and sorrow slumber
At the sight of the beauty that greets them, for
                the charm they have broken.

                                    ROBERT BRIDGES

THE SNOWFLAKE

What heart could have thought you?
Past our devisal
(O filigree petal!)
Fashioned so purely,
Fragilely, surely,
From what Paradisal
Imagineless metal,
Too costly for cost?
Who hammered you, wrought you,
From argentine vapour? ~
"God was my shaper".

Passing surmisal
He hammered, He wrought me,
From curled silver vapour,
To lust of His mind: ~
Thou couldst not have thought me!
So purely, so palely,
Tinily, surely,
Mightily, frailly,
Insculped and embossed,
With His Hammer of wind.
And His graver of frost."

FRANCIS THOMPSON

98

Nature
is full of genius,
full of the divinity;
so that not a snowflake
escapes its fashioning
hand.

HENRY DAVID THOREAU

AND IN THE FROSTY SEASON

when the sun
Was set, and visible for many a mile
The cottage windows blazed through twilight gloom,
I heeded not their summons: happy time
It was for all of us ~ for me
It was a time of rapture! Clear and loud
The village clock tolled six, ~ I wheeled about,
Proud and exulting like an untired horse
That cares not for his home. All shod with steel,
We hissed along the polished ice in games
Confederate, imitative of the chase
And woodland pleasures, ~ the resounding horn
The pack loud chiming, and the hunted hare.
So through the darkness and the cold we flew,
And not a voice was idle; with the din
Smitten, the precipices rang aloud;

The leafless trees and every icy crag
Tinkled like iron; while far distant hills
Into the tumult sent an alien sound
Of melancholy not unnoticed, while the stars
Eastward were sparkling clear, and in the west
The orange sky of evening died away.
Not seldom from the uproar I retired
Into a silent bay, or sportively
Glanced sideway, leaving the tumultuous throng,
To cut across the reflex of a star
That fled, and, flying still before me, gleamed
Upon the glassy plain; and oftentimes,
When we had given our bodies to the wind,
And all the shadowy banks on either side
Came sweeping through the darkness, spinning still
The rapid line of motion, then at once
Have I, reclining back upon my heels,
Stopped short. Yet still the solitary cliffs
Wheeled by me ~ even as if the earth had rolled
With visible motion her diurnal round.
Behind me did they stretch in solemn train,
Feebler and feebler, and I stood and watched
Till all was tranquil as a dreamless sleep...

from "The Prelude" by William Wordsworth

101

THE SNOW-STORM

Announced by all the trumpets of the sky,
Arrives the snow, and, driving o'er the fields,
Seems nowhere to alight: the whited air
Hides hills and woods, the river, and the heaven,
And veils the farmhouse at the garden's end.
The sled and traveller stopped, the courier's feet
Delayed, all friends shut out, the housemates sit
Around the radiant fireplace, enclosed
In a tumultuous privacy of storm.

Come see the north wind's masonry
Out of an unseen quarry evermore
Furnished with tile, the fierce artificer
Curves his white bastions with projected roof
Round every windward stake, or tree, or door.
Speeding, the myriad-handed, his wild work
So fanciful, so savage, nought cares he
For number or proportion. Mockingly,
On coop or kennel he hangs Parian wreaths;

A swan-like form invests the hidden thorn;
Fills up the farmer's lane from wall to wall,
Maugre the farmer's sighs; and at the gate
A tapering turret overtops the work.
And when his hours are numbered, and the world
Is all his own, retiring, as he were not,
Leaves, when the sun appears, astonished Art
To mimic in slow structures, stone by stone,
Built in an age, the mad wind's night-work,
The frolic architecture of the snow.

Ralph Waldo Emerson.

WINTER

When icicles hang by the wall
And Dick the Shepherd blows his nail,
    And Tom bears logs into the hall,
And milk comes frozen home in pail;
    When blood is nipt, and ways be foul,
Then nightly sings the staring owl
            Tuwhoo!
    Tuwhit! tuwhoo! A merry note!
While greasy Joan doth keel the pot.

    When all around the wind doth blow,
And coughing drowns the parson's saw,
    And birds sit brooding in the snow,
And Marian's nose looks red and raw;
    When roasted crabs hiss in the bowl~
Then nightly sings the staring owl
            Tuwhoo!
    Tuwhit! tuwhoo! A merry note!
While greasy Joan doth keel the pot.

WILLIAM SHAKESPEARE.

104

SNOW

In the gloom of whiteness,
In the great silence of snow,
A child was sighing
And bitterly saying: 'Oh,
They have killed a white bird up
there on her nest,
The down is fluttering from her breast.
And still it fell through that
dusky brightness
On the child crying for the bird of the
snow.

EDWARD THOMAS

105

LONGFELLOW'S CAROL

I heard the bells- on Christ-mas Day Their old fa- mi - liar car — ols play, And mild and sweet the words— re - peat Of peace on- earth,- good will — to men.

106

I thought how, as the day had come,
The belfries of all Christendom
Had roll'd along th' unbroken song
Of peace on earth, good will to men.

And in despair I bow'd my head:
'There is no peace on earth,' I said,
'For hate is strong and mocks the song
Of peace on earth, good will to men.'

Then pealed the bells more loud and deep;
'God is not dead, nor doth he sleep:
The wrong shall fail, the right prevail,
With peace on earth, good will to men.'

HENRY WADSWORTH LONGFELLOW

107

And then on Christmas Eve the British soldiers heard
carols coming from the German trenches.
The firing stopped...
As dawn broke on that Christmas Day of 1914 British
and German soldiers met in 'No-Man's Land'.

SILENT NIGHT, HOLY NIGHT

Si - lent night - ho - ly night, - Dark-ness flies,

all is light. Shep - herds hear - the an — gels sing

Hal - le - lu — jah, hail- the King: Je - sus the Saviour is

he — re! Je - sus the Sa - viour is here!

Stille Nacht! Heilige Nacht!
Alles schläft, einsam wacht
Nur das traute, hochheilige Paar.
Holder Knabe im lockigen Haar.
Schlaf in himmlischer Ruh,
Schlaf in himmlischer Ruh!

Silent night, holiest night,
Guiding star, lend thy light,
See the Eastern Magi bring
Gifts and homage to their King,
Jesus the Saviour is here,
Jesus the Saviour is here.

Stille Nacht! heilige Nacht!
Hirten erst kund gemacht,
Durch der Engel Halleluja
Tönt es laut von fern und nah:
Christ, der Retter, ist da,
Christ, der Retter, ist da!

Silent night, holiest night,
Wondrous star, lend thy light,
With the angels let us sing,
Hallelujah to the King.
Jesus the Saviour is here,
Jesus the Saviour is here.

Stille Nacht! heilige Nacht!
Gottes Sohn, O wie lacht
Lieb' aus deinem göttlichen Mund,
Da uns schlägt die rettende Stund,
Christ, in deiner Geburt,
Christ, in deiner Geburt!

JOSEPH MOHR   FRANZ GRUBER

CHRISTMAS LETTER HOME

Drifting and innocent and like snow,
Now memories tease me, wherever I go,
And I think of the glitter of granite and distances
And against the blue air the lovely and bare trees,
And slippery pavements spangled with delight
Under the needles of a winter's night,
And I remember the dances, with scarf and cane,
Strolling home in the cold with the silly refrain
Of a tune by Cole Porter or Irving Berlin
Warming a naughty memory up like gin,
And Bunny and Sheila and Joyce and Rosemary
Chattering on sofas or preparing tea,
With their delicate voices and their small white hands,

This is the sorrow everyone understands.
More than Rostov's artillery, more than the planes
Skirting the cyclonic islands, this remains,
The little, lovely taste of youth we had:
The guns and not our silliness were mad,
All the unloved and ugly seeking power
Were mad, and not our trivial evening hour
Of swirling taffetas and muslin girls,
Oh, not their hands, their profiles, or their curls,
Oh, not the evenings of coffee and sherry and snow,
Oh, not the music. Let us rise and go —
But then the months and oceans lie between,
And once again the dust of spring, the green
Bright beaks of buds upon the poplar trees,
And summer's strawberries, and autumn's ease,
And all the marble gestures of the dead,
Before my eyes caress again your head,
Your tiny strawberry mouth, your bell of hair,
Your blue eyes with their deep and shallow stare,
Before your hand upon my arm can still
The nerves that everything but home makes ill:

In this historic poster-world I move,
Noise, movement, emptiness, but never love,
Yet all this grief we had to have my dear,
And most who grieve have never known, I fear,
The lucky streak for which we die and live,
And to the luckless must the lucky give
All trust, all energy, whatever lies
Under the anger of democracies:
Whatever strikes the towering torturer down,
Whatever can outface the bully's frown,
Talk to the stammerer, spare a cigarette
For tramps at midnight...oh defend it yet!
Some Christmas I shall meet you. Oh, and then
Though all the boys you used to like are men,
Though all my girls are married, though my verse
Has pretty steadily been growing worse,
We shall be happy: we shall smile and say,
'These years! It only seems like yesterday
I saw you sitting in that very chair.'
'You have not changed the way you do your hair.'

'These years were painful, then?' I hardly know.
Something lies gently over them, like snow,
A sort of numbing white forgetfulness...'

And so, goodnight, this Christmas,
                    and God bless!

Written during the second World War by G.S. FRASER

CHRISTMAS AT SEA

The sheets were frozen hard, and they cut the naked hand;
The decks were like a slide, where a seaman scarce could stand,
The wind was a nor'-wester, blowing squally off the sea;
And cliffs and spouting breakers were the only things a-lee.

They heard the surf a-roaring before the break of day;
But t'was only with the peep of light we saw how ill we lay.
We tumbled every hand on deck instanter, with a shout,
And we gave her the maintops'l, and stood by to go about.

All day we tack'd and tack'd between the South Head and the North
All day we haul'd the frozen sheets, and got no further forth;
All day as cold as charity, in bitter pain and dread,
For very life and nature we tack'd from head to head.

We gave the South a wider berth, for there the tide-race roar'd;
But every tack we made we brought the North Head close aboard
So's we saw the cliffs and houses, and the breakers running high,
And the coastguard in his garden, with his glass against his eye

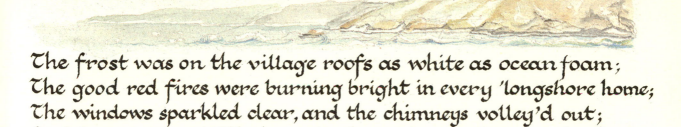

The frost was on the village roofs as white as ocean foam;
The good red fires were burning bright in every 'longshore home;
The windows sparkled clear, and the chimneys volley'd out;
And I vow we sniff'd the victuals as the vessel went about.

The bells upon the church were rung with a mighty jovial cheer;
For it's just that I should tell you how (of all days in the year)
This day of our adversity was blessèd Christmas morn,
And the house above the coastguard's was the house where I was born.

O well I saw the pleasant room, the pleasant faces there,
My mother's silver spectacles, my father's silver hair;
And well I saw the firelight, like a flight of homely elves,
Go dancing round the china-plates that stand upon the shelves!

And well I knew the talk they had, the talk that was of me,
Of the shadow on the household and the son who went to sea;
And O the wicked fool I seemèd, in every kind of way,
To be here and hauling frozen ropes on blessèd Christmas Day.

They lit the high sea-light, and the dark began to fall.
'All hands to loose topgallant sails!' I heard the captain call.
'By the Lord, she'll never stand it,' our first mate Jackson cried.
…'It's the one way or the other, Mr. Jackson', he replied.

She stagger'd to her bearings, but the sails were new and good,
And the ship smelt up to windward just as though she understood.
As the winter's day was ending, in the entry of the night,
We clear'd the weary, headland, and pass'd below the light.

And they heaved a mighty breath, every soul on board but me,
As they saw her nose again pointing handsome out to sea;
But all that I could think of, in the darkness and the cold,
Was just that I was leaving home and my folks were growing old.

ROBERT LOUIS STEVENSON ~

THE HOUSE OF HOSPITALITIES

Here we broached the Christmas barrel,
   Pushed up the charred log-ends;
Here we sang the Christmas carol,
   And called in friends.

Time has tired me since we met here
   When the folk now dead were young,
Since the viands were outset here
   And quaint songs sung.

And the worm has bored the viol
   That used to lead the tune,
Rust eaten out the dial
   That struck night's noon.

Now no Christmas brings in neighbours,
   And the New Year comes unlit;
Where we sang the mole now labours,
   And spiders knit.

Yet at midnight if here walking,
   When the moon sheets wall and tree,
I see forms of old time talking,
   Who smile on me.   THOMAS HARDY

117

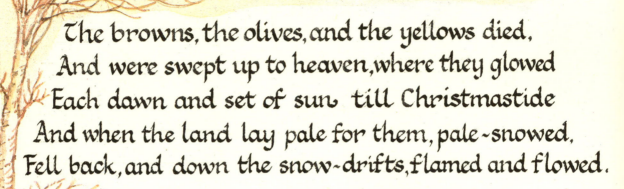

The browns, the olives, and the yellows died,
And were swept up to heaven, where they glowed
Each dawn and set of sun till Christmastide
And when the land lay pale for them, pale-snowed,
Fell back, and down the snow-drifts, flamed and flowed.

From off your face, into the winds of winter,
The sun-brown and the summer-gold are blowing;
But they shall gleam again with spiritual glinter,
When paler beauty on your brows falls, snowing,
And through those snows my looks shall be soft-going.

WINTER SONG   WILFRED OWEN

Mistletoe

Sitting under the mistletoe
(Pale green, fairy mistletoe)
One last candle burning low,
All the sleepy dancers gone,
Just one candle burning on,
Shadows lurking everywhere:
Someone came, and kissed me there.

Tired I was; my head would go
Nodding under the mistletoe
(Pale green, fairy mistletoe)
No footstep came, no voice, but only,
Just as I sat there, sleepy, lonely,
Stooped in the still and shadowy
air,
Lips unseen - and kissed
me there.

WALTER DE LA MARE

119

To the most illustrious
The Contessina Allagia dela Aldobrandeschi
On the Via Martelli, Firenze.

Pontassieve,
Christmas Eve,
Anno Domini 1513.

M
ost noble Contessina,

I salute you. Believe me your most devoted servant. The rascal who carries this letter, if he devour them not on the way, will crave your acceptance of some of the fruits of our garden. Would that the peace of Heaven might reach you through such things of earth. Contessina, forgive an old man's babble. But I am your friend, and my love for you goes deep. There is nothing I can give you which you have not got; but there is much, very much, that, while I cannot give it you can take. No Heaven can come to us unless our hearts find rest in it today. Take Heaven! No peace lies in the future which is not hidden in this present little instant. Take peace. The gloom of the world is but a shadow. Behind it, yet within our reach, is joy. There is radiance and glory in the darkness, could we but see; and to see, we have only to look. Contessina, I beseech you to look.
Life is so generous a giver, but we, judging its gifts by

their covering, cast them away as ugly or heavy or hard. Remove the covering, and you will find beneath it a living splendour, woven of love, by wisdom, with power. Welcome it, grasp it, and you touch the Angel's hand that brings it to you. Everything we call a trial, a sorrow, or a duty: believe me, that angel's hand is there; the gift is there, and the wonder of an over-shadowing Presence. Our joys, too: be not content with them as joys, they too conceal diviner gifts.
Life is so full of meaning and of purpose, so full of beauty ~ beneath its covering ~ that you will find that earth but cloaks your heaven. Courage, then to claim it: that is all! But courage you have: and the knowledge that we are pilgrims together, wending through unknown country, home.
And so, at this Christmas time, I greet you; not quite as the world sends greetings, but with profound esteem, and with the prayer that for you, now and for-ever, the day breaks and the shadows flee away.
I have the honour to be your servant, though the least worthy of them.

Fra Giovanni

121

122

INDEX OF WRITERS AND COMPOSERS

With Dates of Birth and Death, Countries of Birth, and First Lines.